MOM

*moments of
mindfulness*

EDWINA F. BELL, PSY.D.

FREILING
PUBLISHING

Published by Freiling Publishing,
a division of Freiling Agency, LLC.

P.O. Box 1264,
Warrenton, VA 20188

www.FreilingPublishing.com

ISBN 978-1-950948-72-7

Printed in the United States of America

dedication

This book is dedicated to my dearest mom, Mary Francis Hamilton, née Lewis, known by us affectionately as "Babus." I will always carry her wisdom, generosity, and gentle spirit with me. I am glad that God earmarked her to be my mother as He knew exactly what I would need. She showed me the true essence of motherhood and unconditional love of family, for which I am eternally grateful.

table of contents

acknowledgments

First and foremost, I could not have asked for a more devoted family. Thank you to my husband and soul mate, Kevin, for your love, undying support, and encouragement. You have stood with me through all my endeavors, and for this, I am beyond grateful. You are my best friend, and my love for you runs deep. Thank you to my beautiful children Blair and Nia, who love me no matter my shortcomings. I am so impressed by you and truly proud to be your mom. Trust God always, and know that He has great plans for you both!

Thank you, Dad, for your unmatched wisdom, guidance, and sound advice. You have taught me perseverance, determination, and the true meaning of service to others. For your commitment to me and my success, I am eternally thankful. I love you, dad.

To my brother Dwain and sister Carla, I could not have asked for more loving, thoughtful, and passionate siblings (my sibs). I can always count on you to believe in me, and you both are my role models.

I am deeply indebted to my dear friend Michelle, who, without hesitation, took on the task of proofreading and editing my manuscript. Your sagacity, enthusiastic spirit, and invaluable feedback mean more than you could ever know. I could not have done this without you.

Thank you to my dearest friends who have supported me through this journey. Whether it was to provide feedback on the book cover or read a chapter or two, I am humbled and truly blessed to have you in my life.

Last but not least, to my Freiling Publishing team, I can't thank you enough for allowing me the opportunity to write my first book. Your guidance and support have been unparalleled. To you, I am ever so grateful.

priorities

*People often ask me how I keep my priorities
straight in life, and I tell them
that it is done by constantly
straightening them out!*

— JOYCE MEYER

It was 6:36 a.m., and the bus was leaving
at 7:15 a.m. We were stuck in bumper-to-
bumper traffic. There was no way I would
be able to make it across town to arrive at my
daughter's school in time for her to make the
bus. According to the GPS, this was the quickest
route. How could I forget? How could I not
remember? My daughter had talked about this
field trip practically every day since the beginning of the school year. It was the end of the
year field trip. I was praying all the way, while
at the same time beating myself up mentally for
not remembering such an important day for her.
My self-talk went something like, "You're a bad
mom," "How will you make up for this?" and

"You really messed up this time." Once again, it was clear. I needed to re-evaluate my priorities.

Have you ever found yourself in a situation where your priorities were out of order? For me, this was one of those times. What was truly important to me had taken a back seat. Truth be told, my family had taken a back seat to work. I had taken on a new contract, which required a great deal of my time. Work had spilled over into my home life. That meant late nights, and not to mention, I had become more irritable and impatient with my kids, and there seemed to be distance in the relationship with my husband. Needless to say, it was time to revisit my top three priorities: 1) My relationship with God 2) My family and 3) My work, in that order. That meant I needed to look at what was on my plate and, if it didn't align with my priorities, take it off my plate—no ifs, ands, or buts about it. I knew what I needed to do, and once again, that's just what I did.

What are your priorities? Write them down, revisit often, and make any necessary adjustments.

oxygen mask

*I have come to believe that caring
for myself is not self-indulgence.
Caring for myself is an act of survival.*

— AUDRE LORDE

"Should the cabin lose pressure, oxygen masks will drop from the overhead area. Please place the mask over your own mouth and nose before assisting others." If you have ever flown, you know that the flight attendant reviews the safety procedures prior to take-off. You are informed that if there is a loss of cabin pressure, oxygen masks will drop from the overhead area. You are asked to put your oxygen mask on FIRST before assisting others. My initial thought was how selfish, insensitive, and inconsiderate. Take care of your needs first! After much thought, it made perfect sense. How can you be there for others when your own needs are not met? Nonetheless, this is a common problem that impacts many lives.

When you are accustomed to putting others' needs first, it is very challenging to begin the process of even considering yourself, let alone put your needs first. In working with patients over the years, there is a recurring problem when we begin to talk about self-care as an integral part of our day-to-day living. More times than not, the question is asked, "How do I deal with the guilt?" My answer is typically the same, I encourage them to focus on the self-care, not the guilt, and the feelings of guilt will eventually go away. And, they do.

Are you exhausted, overburdened, and stressed? Do you often feel that you have nothing left to give? Could it be that you neglected to put on your oxygen mask? As a mom, you are pulled in many directions, especially if you are a working mom. Life can become so busy that you find yourself indifferent to your personal wants and needs.

When was the last time you put on your oxygen mask FIRST? If you can't remember, it's long overdue. For me, putting on my oxygen mask looks like taking a bike ride, reading a book, listening to one of my favorite tunes, or just sitting and doing nothing. What about you? My only suggestion, don't wait until emotional burnout lessens or feelings of guilt disappear before you put on your oxygen mask. It just may be too late.

Identify one thing you can do today to put on your oxygen mask. Do that one thing TODAY.

apples

> *Every book is a quotation; and every house is a quotation out of all forests, and mines, and stone quarries; and every man is a quotation from all his ancestors.*
>
> — **RALPH WALDO EMERSON**

There she sat—sad, dejected, eyes downcast, in between both of her parents. She appeared childlike, despite being twenty-eight. Her mother had called for an appointment, expressing concerns that her daughter was not doing well. Indeed, it was pretty evident. She was not well and had not been for quite some time. Thankfully, she had come home just in time before things spiraled out of control. Angela had moved across the country years prior to prove that she could do life on her own.

I sat across from them, asking questions primarily of the daughter, who often responded after a brief delay and with much effort. After each response, I observed her father shaking his head repeatedly, seemingly in agreement. I eventually turned to him and inquired about his thoughts. He stated that he knew exactly what his daughter was going through as this had been his existence for some years. Then, he began to cry and expressed that he could finally put a name to what he experienced. It was clinical depression. Although undiagnosed, he believed he had experienced depression on and off throughout his life, and he was certain his father had suffered with it too. He just remembered his family saying that his father had "gone crazy."

Isn't it interesting how we tend to take care of our physical health and neglect our emotional well-being? Did you know that mental health conditions, like medical conditions, can run in families? If you desire to be your best self, it's essential to address your needs from a holistic perspective, including your emotional and mental health.

Start now. Get your mental health screening today. Be on your way to living a better life for yourself and those you care about the most.

got friends?

Who can you count on when you are at your lowest? Who do you rely on for emotional support? Friends, true friends, are there to not only lift you up when you're going through tough times but to help you celebrate when things are going well. Friends are there when nothing is going on at all. Wholesome, genuine friendships can help decrease stress, provide peace of mind, and help you cope better. To be honest, I've had a few bumps in the road when it comes to friendships. For some, we were able to work through it and maintain the friendship. For others, the friendship ended.

Most people desire friendships; however, they frequently allow hurt and disappointment from past relationships to hinder their ability to initiate and maintain current ones. How does one move beyond the past hurts to truly benefit from friendship? Most times, it takes healing from past hurts, forgiveness, and being open to trusting again.

Are you desiring friendship but find yourself holding onto fear of the possibility of getting hurt? Could you be missing out on a healthy and wholesome friendship because of past hurts and disappointments? If your expectation is that friends don't disappoint or let you down, you will find yourself going from relationship to relationship to relationship. When faced with challenges in your relationship with others, express how you feel and work on overcoming obstacles together. Lasting company is not one that is perfect, but one that has been tested and endured despite the test. I challenge you today to not allow the disappointment, pain, and hurt from previous relationships to hinder the opportunity to experience a loving, fulfilling, and wholesome friendship. The kind that if you haven't spoken in quite a while, when you do connect, you pick up where you left off.

Who are your friends? List their names. If there is no one on your list, start with an acquaintance and work on building a friendship.

honor yourself

*The moment you start to wonder
if you deserve better, you do.*

— UNKNOWN

Karen had been in her current relationship for almost ten years. While they
had good times, what stuck with her
the most was the belittling remarks, put-downs,
disrespect, and disregard. She felt unloved,
unappreciated, and undervalued. She had
become isolated from her friends and family yet
she continued to rationalize why being in the
relationship wasn't so bad. In fact, Karen had
been from one abusive relationship to another.
A pattern had been established. The emotional
and verbal abuse had become more and more
apparent. She began to believe that she was the
one to be blamed for the relationship being the
way it was. Karen had tried to make it work. She
knew if she could just be a little kinder, more
considerate, or not as vocal, their relationship
would improve, and her partner would finally

realize that she was worthy of love. This seemed to work, but only for a short time then things went back to normal. She did that for many years until she began to lose herself little by little. When Karen showed up in my office, she did not recognize herself or who she had become.

Are you in a relationship which you know deep down inside is not healthy for you? Do you know you deserve better? Ask yourself the question, "How am I honoring myself in this relationship?" Am I being valued, supported, and appreciated? Getting out of an unhealthy relationship may not be the easiest thing to do. Patients I have worked with have often expressed holding onto hope that the other person will change as the reason they remain. I challenge you to take your focus off the other person and put effort into the personal change that leads to you seeing yourself as valuable, lovable, and worthy of the best.

Do a self-assessment of your relationship. Ask yourself, "How am I honoring myself?" If you are in an abusive relationship, seek help today!

forgiveness is for you

*I think the first step is to understand that
forgiveness does not exonerate the perpetrator.
Forgiveness liberates the victim.
It's a gift you give yourself.*

—T. D. JAKES

Forgive? No way! I can't! According to Merriam-Webster dictionary, the definition of forgiveness is 'to cease to feel resentment against' and to 'to grant relief...' I'm sure you have heard people say that forgiveness is for you, not the other person. There is truth to this. Forgiveness can provide peace of mind, freedom, and hope.

While forgiveness is for you, let's be honest, it's not always easy to forgive. When you have been hurt deeply, especially by those you love, it can be difficult to let go of the hurt and the pain from the past. Any thought or memory of what happened seems to set off and evoke unpleasant feelings. What can make it even more challenging is seeing the one who hurt you living a seemingly happy and fulfilling life. Do you feel stuck, stuck in unforgiveness?

Moving beyond unforgiveness means recognizing the importance of YOU acknowledging what was said or done, despite others' tendency to minimize. While people may encourage you to "just move one," realize that forgiveness takes time. Grant yourself time and patience to work through your feelings. Identify them. Do you feel rejected, angry, or sad? Be intentional about acknowledging your feelings. Be specific in identifying what was done to you. Don't sugarcoat it. Be honest with yourself. When reminded, tell yourself, "I have forgiven that person, and I am moving on." Just know that as time passes, while you may not forget what happened, the emotional toll it takes will begin to lessen. You may not forget, but you will find peace in letting go of negative feelings that have kept you weighed down and hindered your ability to move forward.

Who do you need to forgive? Make a list today. Remember, forgiveness is for you, not the other person.

find the faith
to let go

*The highest privilege and purpose as a parent
is to lead the child in the way of Christ.*

— MAX LUCADO

My son was nine-years-old at the time. He had spent time with friends in the neighborhood, playing video games. It was mid-day, and we were preparing to leave the house to run errands. He came to me and mentioned that he left one of his video games at his friend's house and wanted to retrieve it before leaving. Upon returning, I could tell by the look on his face that he was upset. His friends said that they did not have the game. Yet, he knew that he had left it there. He was convinced that one of them had to have it.

If you're like me, there are times you want to intervene in your child's life and solve all of their problems. You know, though, that there are lessons that they must learn on their own. I wanted to go there and demand that one of them return the game or else. Of course, that's not what I did. I saw a much better option. I grabbed my son's hands and began to pray. I asked the Lord to convict the heart of the person who had the video game and return it. Then, we left the house and enjoyed our time together.

Upon returning home from running errands, my son jumped out of the car and, with excitement in his eyes, ran to the front door. With a big smile on his face, he held the video game in his hand. He exclaimed, "They returned it! They returned it!" I reminded him that God had answered his prayer and convicted hearts. And that he should always remember to pray about everything.

As a mother, what beliefs and values would you like to pass on to your children? Start today.

learn to say no

*It's only by saying 'no' that you can concentrate
on the things that are really important.*

— STEVE JOBS

'NO' is such a small yet powerful word!
A word, if exercised, can provide
freedom from stress, peace, and
contentment beyond measure. Yet, saying "no"
can be difficult, especially when you are not
accustomed to saying "no."

Do you often say "yes" when you wished you
had said "no?" For me and many others, this
has become one of the most challenging exercises. In treating patients over the years, helping
them to say 'no' to the things they don't want
and "yes" to the things they do, has more times
than not become the focus of our work together.
Some expressed fear if they were to say "no,"
others would not love them, or somehow the
world would fall apart. They were uneasy about
how others would respond, especially since they
saw themselves as a people-pleaser, rarely, if at

all, saying "no." For others, it had been a habit, something they were used to. Saying "no" wasn't even thought of as an option. How does one say "no" when others are used to them saying 'yes?'

Let's be honest; habits can be challenging to break. If saying "yes" has become a habit, where do you even start to break the habit? How do you change? I have found that in working with patients, it takes time and patience. I have also found that one simple statement can help start the process. This one exercise has been beneficial in helping one to become comfortable with saying "no." Try it. When someone asks you to do something or asks a favor of you, I want you to stop, take a deep breath, and say, "Let me think about it." By doing so, you have time to honestly think about whether or not this is something you would like to do. As you contemplate, ask yourself the question, "What will this require of me?" and "Is this something that I really want to do?" The question is not can you do it, but do you want to do it. The more you exercise saying "no," the easier it becomes, and the more, as Steve Jobs said, "you can focus on the things that are important to you."

Try it. When someone asks something of you, stop and say, "Let me think about it." Be sure to get back to them about your decision.

a call to action

Seek help today. Don't delay. My motto is: when in doubt, get checked out!

— DR. EDWINA F. BELL

D o you know your mental health status? Many people do not make their mental and emotional well-being a priority for various reasons. Some of these include miseducation about what mental illness is, fear of others perceiving them as "crazy," not knowing what to expect if seen by a mental health professional, and cultural barriers, to name a few. Despite these concerns, statistics indicate that one in five Americans will experience a mental health condition annually. Mental illness does not discriminate. No matter what the barrier, an individual's mental and emotional health matters.

Knowing the signs and symptoms of mental illness is critical. Interestingly, a person may be experiencing emotional challenges and not even be aware that it's mental health-related. I have worked with patients at the suggestion of friends and family who noticed a difference in their functioning. Other patients have come reporting that they just weren't feeling well; they weren't themselves. There are a variety of reasons people seek mental health services.

Not everyone I see is diagnosed with a major mental health condition such as bipolar disorder, major depression, or schizophrenia, for example. I also work with patients who are experiencing stress due to life's transitions, grieving due to loss, and those who desire to work on more effective time management. Whatever the circumstance, they all come seeking answers and guidance on how to improve their mental and emotional well-being.

If you or someone you know may be experiencing a mental health condition, don't delay; seek help today! When in doubt, get checked out.

Resources

National Suicide Prevention Lifeline 1-800-273-TALK (8255) For Deaf and Hard of Hearing call 1-800-799-4889

Text HOME to 741741

www.suicidepreventionlifeline.org

If you are unable to speak safely, you can log onto thehotline.org.

***IF YOU ARE IN AN EMERGENCY
SITUATION, PLEASE CALL 911***

it takes a village

It takes a village to raise a child.

— AFRICAN PROVERB

Rearing children, while gratifying, can be very challenging. I was grateful to have my mother and brother-in-law's mother to help care for my son when he was younger. In fact, they helped take care of my son and his cousin; they were born six weeks apart. Despite my village, there were times that were difficult, like the time my husband won a trip on his job to Puerto Rico. While I was excited and looking forward to the trip, I struggled with leaving our son because he was having difficulty transitioning from being breastfed to the bottle. In preparation for the trip, I had started the transition early. Nonetheless, he was outright refusing! My mother encouraged me to go, reminding me that he will eat when he gets hungry. Still, I worried. What if he doesn't eat? What if he starves to death? What if he cries all day and all night? With much trepidation, I went on the trip with my husband. And my mother was right! No surprise. My son was just fine. I remember calling back home and my mother answering the phone as she held him while he fed on the bottle—what a relief.

My village started with those closest to me, my mother and my sister's mother-in-law. Over the years, I have grown my village by talking with other moms at my children's school and those within my church community. I have gleaned so much by swapping stories and sharing what has and has not worked. I found that talking with others has helped to normalize my experiences and prevent isolation, especially when my children were much younger. Connecting with others has also allowed me the opportunity to nurture self-care, whether it's going to lunch or being part of a book club.

I don't know what I would do without my village. For me, it's been a vital necessity. I have found that over the years, as my children have gotten older, what I need from my village has changed. While I no longer need someone to watch my children while I run an errand, I need a listening ear and someone who can be in prayer with me over my children. I need fellowship with other like-minded women. I need women who I can share in their celebration of their children's accomplishments and advice from those who have "been there." Who is in your village? We all need one. If you are looking to grow your village, my suggestion starts with what's in your hand.

Identify who is in your village. If you don't have anyone, think about who you would like to build a relationship with. Invite them in.

in the stillness

*Learning how to be still, to really be still
and let life happen — that stillness
becomes a radiance.*

— MORGAN FREEMAN

In the darkness, I find tranquility. In the stillness of the morning, when the kids are asleep, and there is no hustle and bustle, that's where I find peace and serenity. Although I'm typically not a morning person, the benefits of waking up early have outweighed the temptation to stay in bed. It's quiet. In the stillness of the morning, I find clarity, answers, and equilibrium. It's during this time that I pray and meditate.

For me, prayer and meditation in the early morning at the break of dawn provide a sense of inner peace and help me feel at ease. It is during this time that I seek direction and find clarity and answers to my petitions. I recall when my mother had taken ill and had to be hospitalized. We were praying for guidance and answers as to the next steps in how to care for her. One morning, a physician who I knew through my father and brother came across my mind. I saw him vividly. I made a note of it; however, I did not think much of it and went about my day. The clarity came when I was talking with my brother a few hours later, and he mentioned that he was going to contact the same physician who had crossed my mind early that morning. That was the clarity and confirmation we needed regarding the next step in taking care of our mother!

There are many benefits to stillness. Stillness is good for one's physical, mental, and spiritual well-being. For me, I have found direction when I am confused about which way to turn. I have found restoration and healing. I have also found gratitude. When I am intentional about being still, I can focus on what I have rather than what I don't have.

Where do you find clarity, peace of mind, and gratitude? Be intentional about setting aside time to be still, to step away from the day-to-day hustle and bustle. There is restorative healing, clarity of thought, and resoluteness in stillness.

Be intentional. Find stillness.

nobody's a mind reader

Ask for what you want,
and be prepared to get it.

— MAYA ANGELOU

Wouldn't life be easier if we could read people's minds? To some degree, we all expect others to treat us the way we treat them. We want others to be considerate, keep in touch, and to ask how we are doing from time to time. If we are honest with ourselves, we enter into a relationship with expectations that at times are not met. What happens when our expectations are unmet? What happens when how you treat others is not reciprocated?

In working with patients over the years, often, the challenge has been what to do when expectations are unmet. There appears to be this notion that others should know what we want and need. Isn't it obvious? What may be obvious to us may not be so apparent to someone else. Unfortunately, this has led to frustration and disappointment merely because we expect others to be mind readers.

Once we realize that no one is a mind reader, we can begin to focus on what we can do to get our own needs met. We can start to shift control from external to internal. Often, it's a matter of finding and exercising your voice. Aha! While this may sound easy for some, others find it rather difficult, especially when asking for what you need is not something you are accustomed to doing or when people-pleasing is always what you have done. Just the thought of asking for what you want stirs up fear and apprehension.

How do you overcome the fear of asking for what you want and need? You have to start by doing; just ask. If you focus on fear, it won't happen. Try exercising your voice despite how afraid you might feel. You may find that the fear begins to dissipate the more you ask. You will find that the world doesn't fall apart. You may get resistance from others who are not used to you exercising your voice. That's to be expected, but don't let it stop you. Remember, no one is a mind reader.

Start the process of asking for what you want and need. Begin today.

year-round cleaning

I am a believer that eventually,
everything comes back to you.
You get back what you give out.

— NANCY REAGAN

As a little girl, I remember looking through my closet and dresser for clothes that I had outgrown. I would try them on, and the ones that didn't fit my mother would pack them up to be given to those in need. This occurred throughout the year, without fail. I never really understood the impact of this until I got older. In retrospect, I know for sure that my siblings and I were well taken care of and never went without. It was not until I became an adult that I fully understood the concept that what you give away will come back to you. Now, I truly appreciate the lesson that my mother was instilling in us.

The concept of sowing and reaping is undeniable. As my mother did, I too continue this practice of sowing with my children. It never fails. This one particular memory stands out. It was maybe a few days after my children had given to others in need that they received a box full of clothes from their Nanny. What you put out into the world, you will receive. While you may not see a return immediately, just wait; it's coming. Ask yourself this question, "Is what you put out there what you want?"

Think about it. What is it that you need to give away? Is it more love, more understanding, more compassion, more forgiveness? Maybe you have been holding onto things that you know you will never use. Try giving them away. Believe it or not, there are benefits to decluttering. Getting rid of things is not only good for your environment but your mind. It provides peace, clarity, and simplicity. I have come to know for sure that whatever you give away has a way of coming back to you. Interesting how that works.

What's on your agenda to sow today?

baggage

*The things you want are always possible;
it is just that the way to get them is
not always apparent. The only real obstacle
in your path to a fulfilling life is you,
and that can be a considerable obstacle
because you carry the baggage of
insecurities and past experience.*

— LES BROWN

Do you really want to move forward? What are you willing to let go of? I have been fortunate to work with many patients over the years who are resilient and strong, yet vulnerable enough to allow themselves the opportunity to grow, knowing that part of their growth lies in letting go of baggage from their past. Some patients come needing to move beyond unresolved issues in the relationship with their parents, some to resolve past hurts and disappointments, and others to let go of unforgiveness. While letting go can be challenging and painful, it is necessary to experience peace, contentment, and satisfaction.

Did you know that holding onto baggage from the past can impact your physical and mental health? What we think impacts how we feel and ultimately, how we behave. Harboring negative feelings of anger, resentment, and bitterness can especially keep you weighed down and feeling low. It can impact your relationships. It can rob you of gratitude. It can hinder you from enjoying the present moment.

How does one even begin to let go of excess baggage from the past? Acknowledge your feelings that you have attached to the situation. By acknowledging them, you weaken the power the situation has over you. Think about how you might re-describe the effect of the situation from negative to positive. Perhaps growing up with an absent parent helped you realize the importance of friendships in your life. Be patient and kind to yourself. Be mindful not to pick it up once you've placed it down. Remind yourself, "I'm moving on....." There are no guarantees that you will forget what happened to you. However, when you think about it, you can put it in its proper place which is behind you.

Which baggage will you put down today?

juggling act

Working mothers' laughter comes hardest when
our double life is revealed for what it is:
A juggling act in which the balls can drop
at any time, invariably on our own head.

— ALLISON PEARSON

I was no exception. In mid-March 2020, like many others, I transitioned from working face-to-face in my office to working virtually from home. The transition was necessary due to safety issues and uncertainties surrounding the COVID-19 pandemic. At that time, I did not know what the transition would bring I just knew I had no choice in the matter. Here I am, over a year later, still working from home.

I'll be honest, the transition was tough initially. It came with losses, changes and definitely new and unexpected responsibilities. I missed being in the office seeing patients face-to-face. I missed the freedom to go outside without concern as to the implications, primarily physical. I missed being able to socialize and engage with others outside of my home. Times had changed and rather abruptly. The way we used to operate had become a thing of the past.

I was not only working from home but I was also supporting my daughter in her online schooling; hence the juggling act. I had taken on new roles, including the lunch lady, IT technician, and PE coach, to name a few. The old routine was no longer relevant; a new one had to be created. This required patience and flexibility. Patience with myself and with my daughter who was also trying to process what was happening while at the same time being required to do her best in school and move forward, isolated from friends.

As I look back, while I am by no means an expert juggler, I have found a few things that have helped to manage my life and my schedule. I have learned the importance of being flexible. What worked one day, didn't work so well the next and that was okay. I have become more intentional about taking care of myself. One way I have done this is by stepping away and pressing the reset button. This helped me to understand the importance of extending grace to myself and to others. Ultimately, what has helped me the most is knowing there are things in life that I can control and those that I cannot.

Identify one thing that can help you to manage your life better from day-to-day.

out of the mouth

Words have a magical power.
They can either bring the greatest happiness
or the deepest despair.

— SIGMUND FREUD

Have you ever been around someone and found yourself beginning to feel bad? You felt good before you met with them and then after you left, your mood was down and you just didn't feel good. You realized it was not the person, necessarily; it was what they said. It was what came out of their mouth. Practically every word was negative, pessimistic, or critical. They tended to see the glass half empty rather than half full.

Did you know the words you speak are powerful? Words carry energy. Words can create a person's existence. Words impact our thoughts, how we feel, and how we behave. Words not only affect the speaker but affect the receiver as well. What you speak can influence others greatly;

hence, the impact of orators, motivational speakers, and the like.

Words have their root in our past. We are what we speak partly because of how we were spoken to and the messages imparted. If you were told you are worthless, not good enough, or lazy, you might find yourself acting that way. On the other hand, words of affirmation such as you are important, you matter, and you are valued feel differently and will likely cause you to behave in a contrasting manner. As children, we take in whatever our environment gives us. We do not have a choice. The good thing about growth and maturity is that it comes with choice.

Irrespective of the words spoken to you in the past or the messages you have carried along the way, choose to speak words that encourage, strengthen, and edify. Watch how others respond to you. It may just make the difference in your thinking, how you feel, and ultimately your reality. A change in your words can make all the difference.

I challenge you today, choose to speak positively.

passed down

Self-care is not about self-indulgence;
it's about self-preservation.

— AUDREY LORDE

Every summer as a child, my mom, siblings, and I would visit her family in Ohio. This ritual became something I looked forward to yearly. The days were full of fun, from sunup to sundown. We spent the majority of time outdoors, running, laughing, and playing. The time spent with our cousins is one of my fondest childhood memories.

In preparation for our trip, my mom would always pack early. By the time it came for our departure, we were ready with all that we needed and more. Aside from our clothes and toiletries, there was one item that was a necessity for my mom. She made sure she had several word search puzzle books for the plane ride to Ohio. As soon as we got on the plane, fastened our seatbelts, and took off, my mom pulled out her word search puzzles, sat back and relaxed the rest of the flight. As a child, I would watch my mom, not really understanding the benefit of what she was doing. This was just something she did. As I have gotten older, I realized that she was passing down something of great value.

In retrospect, I understand this was one of the ways my mom took care of herself. She was taking time to engage in what she found relaxing and pleasurable. This reminds me of the times we would work on jigsaw puzzles together. If you have ever worked on a jigsaw puzzle, you know how relaxing it can be. I truly enjoyed this time with my mom. I am grateful for the lessons she passed down, especially those that have helped bolster my mental and emotional well-being.

What is it that you would like to give to the next generation? Start today.

internal or external?

One of the most difficult things is not to change
society — but to change yourself.

— NELSON MANDELA

Jason said he was done! If this didn't work, it was over! He showed up to my office frustrated and at his wit's end. He was adamant about needing to change his spouse, which he said would solve all of their problems. He reiterated, if she would only just change, the issues in their relationship would be solved. Jason was intent on changing his wife. He emphasized this was his last attempt to salvage their relationship.

As we began our work together, Jason found himself becoming more and more frustrated; not because his wife wasn't changing, but because HE was changing. Interestingly, his frustrations had nothing to do with his wife. In fact, the focus had shifted from his wife to

himself. Jason's aha moment was when he realized he had the power to change the relationship
with his wife by changing what he truly had the
control to change, himself! He had for so many
years and in different relationships, focused on
changing the other person. Now, it was time to
do some introspection and focus on changing
himself.

Do you find yourself going from relationship to relationship, frustrated and unhappy?
Are you intent on changing the other person?
Why not try focusing on what you can control.
Just like Jason, you too can begin the process of
changing your relationship with others by identifying areas of personal growth. For Jason, his
growth areas focused on listening more, being
patient, and acceptance. He would often listen
to respond rather than listen to understand and
relate. He also understood that he was rather
impatient, as many had told him so over the
years. Patience was not his strong suit. At the
end of the day, Jason knew that his main goal
was to work on accepting people for who they
are; he had work to do.

**What is one growth area that you need to work
on?**

stressed?

As you grow older, you will discover that you have two hands. One for helping yourself, the other for helping others.

— AUDREY HEPBURN

I have been rather fortunate to work with brave and courageous individuals during my years in private practice. Many are individuals like you who have committed to making improvements in their lives by facing life's challenges, some with bravery and boldness and others with trepidation. Nonetheless, they faced them—men and women who decided to move forward on their journey to get to know themselves better and become better.

In thinking about these men and women, a recurring theme was to help identify ways to manage stress more effectively. The source of the stress varied from job-related, to familial, and to parental, yet all had stress. Many times, the referrals came from physicians, who were the first point of contact. Physicians who understood that a big part of their patient's well-being had to do with them addressing their emotional needs. I welcome these referrals because I understand the mind-body connection and how physical health conditions can be stress-related. More importantly, helping patients understand how taking care of their emotional well-being may lead to physical health improvements is vital.

There is this one particular patient who comes to mind. She was taking care of her elderly mother. Although she had siblings, she was the primary caretaker. She was not only a caretaker, but she was also a business owner, a spouse, and a mother, to mention a few of her roles. At times, she was able to manage her stress better than others. However, stress was taking a toll on her overall health status. She had a history of hypertension, which she believed was under control until she visited her cardiologist who reported that it was not. She knew that she was stressed out; however, she just did not realize how much it affected her physical health. This is where I came to meet Jennifer, referred by her cardiologist for stress management strategies.

In working with patients over the years, one strategy that is beneficial in reducing stress levels is identifying and focusing on what one can control. Patients have also benefited from implementing self-care strategies, such as deep breathing exercises, meditation, and engaging in pleasurable activities, despite feelings of guilt for taking care of themselves. This was particularly helpful for caretakers and mothers. They realized that as they continued to engage in self-care, the guilty feelings seemed to wane, along with the stress.

What do you do to manage stress?

what do you think?

*The most courageous act is still to think
for yourself. Aloud.*

— COCO CHANEL

Kimberly had not told anyone about her appointment with me. She was very hesitant because, in her culture, you only saw a "shrink" if you were "crazy." She did not want to be perceived as "crazy." Kimberly was always told to solve her problems by seeking prayer and "wisdom from on high." But, she had done that. She had done that over and over and over again, and nothing changed. She woke up daily feeling sad, discouraged, and down. She thought maybe it was hormonal. She thought that if she lightened her load at work that she would feel better. Another month had passed, and she was able to decrease her workload. Even so doing, she felt the same. If anything, the days became more difficult and challenging to face.

Kimberly had grown up in a household where you don't share your family secrets. It was all about "saving face." What happened in Kimberly's house stayed in Kimberly's house; to share was like betrayal. Consequently, Kimberly suffered in silence.

Sound familiar? Throughout our time together, Kimberly would often emphasize what others thought about various situations and circumstances. I, in turn, would ask, "What do you think?" She eventually shared with one of her closest friends the challenges she was experiencing to elicit understanding and build a much-needed support system. This was a big step for Kimberly. Interestingly, Kimberly's friend shared that she too had been struggling with some of the same issues.

Do you ever place others' thoughts and perceptions about your situation before your own? Do you put your needs on the back burner because of what others may think if they knew or found out? I challenge you to move forward in what you think is best for you.

Ask yourself, "What do I think?"

self-love

*The more you give to yourself,
the more love you have to give to others,
and the more value you can add to the world.*

— UNKNOWN

How can you love others when you don't love yourself? If one demonstrates hate toward others, does that mean that they don't have self-love?

There are many ways to practice self-love. One way is to honor yourself in your relationships. Be true to yourself. Value yourself by ensuring that your relationships are the essence of how you want and deserve to be treated. This may not necessarily be the way you were treated in the past or the way you are being treated in your current relationships. Make the change that is necessary and long overdue.

Demonstrate self-love by extending an olive branch to self. Maybe you are dissatisfied because of circumstances that have happened in your past, or maybe things are just not working out the way you had envisioned. Whatever the unhappiness or displeasure, make peace with yourself by putting the past behind you so that you can enjoy the present and look to the future with optimism. Change what you can about your current situation and work on letting go of those things that have already happened and cannot be changed.

Love yourself by staying away from the comparison trap. When you compare yourself to others, you fail to recognize what makes you a unique individual. You have a unique set of qualities and characteristics that are unlike any other. Demonstrate self-love by being your authentic self; unapologetically and with no comparisons.

Do you struggle to love others? Do you struggle to be kind toward others? Could it be that you don't love yourself? The only way to truly love others is to love yourself first. Remember, it's easier to give what you already have.

Got love? If no, start by demonstrating self-love.

can you see it?

Every great dream begins with a dreamer.
Always remember, you have within you
the strength, the patience, and the passion
to reach for the stars to change the world.

— HARRIET TUBMAN

What are your ambitions? What are your goals? Do you have dreams and aspirations that have not been actualized? Effective change begins in your mind. What you focus on grows in your mind. Visualization is known to be effective in one accomplishing their dreams and desires.

Visualization can help you to move closer to reaching your dreams, goals, and aspirations. How does one utilize visualization to bring about change? Visualization involves spending time alone. Sit, close your eyes, and see yourself attaining your goal. Imagine yourself as if you had achieved your goal—as if you were living your dream. Tap into all of your senses. Create a detailed image utilizing all your senses. What do you see? Is there an audience? What does your sense of smell capture? What does it feel like? Are there sounds, colors?

Visualization combined with action leads to success. Once you have created a visual image, think about one action that you can take to move you closer to your dream. Complete the action that will move you one step closer to your goal. Identify as many steps as needed and complete them.

In addition to visualization, it is vital that you BELIEVE you can achieve your dreams and goals. You must accept it to be true, that without a doubt, what you desire will become a reality. Remember, despite what others may say or how absurd they may think of the idea, it is for you to see it, act on it, and believe it.

Practice visualization to make your ambitions and dreams a reality.

what's your connection?

Loneliness does not come from having no people around you, but from being unable to communicate the things that seem important to you.

— CARL JUNG

Longevity and socialization; there is a connection. Those who engage in good quality intimate relationships tend to be happier and live longer. Is your communication style conducive to maintaining healthy relationships with others? Effective communication can enhance a relationship and clear up any misunderstandings. Effective communication is a skill that can be taught. The challenge becomes not what you know but using what you know and putting it into practice.

Communication is best received when both parties are calm and rational, rather than angry and upset. If you find yourself frustrated and upset, taking time out to regroup is likely the next best step. Let the other person know that you need a time out but that you will be back. I would suggest you schedule a time to have a follow-up conversation, preferably by the end of the day.

Effective communication skills can be learned. In my work with couples and individuals, I have found that people often listen in order to respond rather than to understand and relate. Have you ever been talking with someone and before they finished, you knew exactly what you wanted to say? It's likely because you were not listening actively. To listen with intention is to pay attention purposely and to understand the entire message of what the other person is relaying. This is what active listening looks like.

What happens if what the other person says is confusing and unclear? Ask for clarification. You might say something like, "Let me make sure I understand what you are saying. Are you saying......?" This is a technique that helps strengthen one's communication skills. Another helpful tip for effective communication is to utilize "I statements." For example, you might say, "I feel......when you......" This allows the other person to receive what you are saying with an open mind. Just remember, effective communication skills can be learned. It's not whether or not you are teachable, but whether you utilize the skills taught.

Strengthen your relationships by implementing one effective communication tip today.

what are you sowing?

The best way to find yourself is to lose yourself in the service of others.

— MAHATMA GANDHI

If you have never volunteered, I encourage you to start today. Volunteering has many benefits from a holistic perspective. It meets one's spiritual, physical, and emotional needs. Volunteering is a selfless act that meets the needs of both receiver and giver.

In giving back, you have the opportunity to see your life from a different lens. It's amazing how your focus shifts from what you don't have to what you do. I don't know about you, but volunteering helps to activate a heart of gratitude. It allows us to shift our focus from any wants or desires that we have for the future to gratitude in the present moment. If you are struggling to stay in the moment and appreciate what you have, try volunteering.

Volunteering helps to engender sensitivity and compassion toward others. In turn, there are benefits to one's physical and emotional well-being. When you help to relieve another person's suffering and hardship, you feel good. There is a sense of satisfaction and contentment. To volunteer is to connect humans on a deeper level of compassion. I even read where volunteering aids to boost one's immune system and lower stress levels. The benefits are endless.

Lastly, and this one I believe is the most important, volunteering can allow you to be a generational changer. My daughter, who volunteered to help in the distribution of turkeys one year, mentioned how good it made her feel that she could give to others who did not have food. She also shared how giving is important because you never know one day you may be in need. At such a young age, she understood that you treat others like you would want to be treated because "one day that could be you in need."

What is one way you can give back? Start today.

difficult people

*In life, we will always encounter
difficult people. Don't allow them to frustrate
you or steal your joy.*

— VICTORIA OSTEEN

How do you deal with difficult people? People you want to avoid at all costs. People who, when you see them, cause you to want to turn and run the other way. How do you deal with difficult people with whom you work, live or interact with on a daily basis? As much as you may want to stay away and sever the relationship, there are times you just can't. What do you do?

Setting boundaries in a relationship with difficult people can be challenging but necessary. Set limits on how much access you allow them to have. This may mean being respectful yet concise in your interactions with them. When they call, you can choose to answer. If you do, you can decide how long you want to talk. Setting boundaries will provide a sense of control in the matter.

Try not to personalize your interactions with difficult people. Nine times out of ten, the way they are with you is the way they are with everyone else. This is typically confirmed when you listen to what others say about the person. You may even have the opportunity to hear how the person interacts with others. In listening and talking with others, you may find that they feel the same.

Boundaries are a tough one. Accept difficult people for who they are. Accepting, however, does not mean that you allow them to be discourteous or disrespectful toward you. Stand up for yourself in these situations. Express how you think and feel as situations come up, and then move on.

Let's face it, dealing with difficult people can be taxing. Try setting boundaries. Try not to take what they say personally. Ultimately, try to accept them for who they are. At least you will know what to expect.

Who do you need to set boundaries with? Start today.

checkup

Your life is a reflection of your thoughts.
If you change your thinking,
you'll change your life.

— AUTHOR UNKNOWN

Pain, pain, pain! It began at an early age. I remember growing up and my mom taking my siblings and me for our annual physical exams. The exams were comprehensive. The doctor checked our hearing, eyesight, reflexes, and heart, etc. My only question was whether or not I was going to get a shot? At that time, I did not understand the importance of immunization and prevention. Honestly, I really didn't care. I just remember the pain I felt when I got a shot. It hurt!

Nonetheless, it never failed. When the visit was over, and before we left the office, we had an appointment scheduled for our next visit. All of this was necessary and done as a preventative measure to ensure we maintained good physical health.

Being purposeful is taking care of self holistically. It involves addressing one's spiritual, physical, work, social relationships, intimacy, and emotional health. What if you were intentional about taking care of your emotional/ mental health as you do your physical? What would you do differently? Would you schedule a mental health checkup? There are benefits to having emotional wellness checkups.

A mental health checkup can help to manage life better. While you may not be able to prevent life from happening, a mental health checkup can be beneficial in navigating life's challenges more effectively. It can help to improve productivity and the overall quality of your relationships. If your focus is on living life holistically, taking care of your emotional/mental health can help you enjoy your work, relationship with others, and overall life outlook. A mental health checkup can help prevent disease progression. For those with a mental health condition, whether you are aware of it or not, regular mental health checkups can help you develop effective coping skills and tools to manage your condition with confidence and determination. When my kids were younger and were not feeling well, I wouldn't hesitate to contact their pediatrician for advice and guidance. They were the experts. Be proactive and schedule your emotional wellness visit today. Rely on the experts.

Start today in making your emotional well-being a priority.

support

*Many people will walk in and out
of your life, but only true friends will leave
footprints in your heart.*

— ELEANOR ROOSEVELT

The silence was deafening as we got closer. Maria and I were on our way to see the therapist for the initial visit. In my opinion, this was long overdue. It was painful for me to watch one of my dearest friends suffer. Maria had been in a relationship for many years now and was unhappy. The verbal and emotional abuse was taking a toll on her. Our conversations entailed her expressing discontent and me listening. For me, this just didn't seem like enough. There had to be more I could do.

Maria and I had talked about her seeking therapy for quite some time now, and when she called and said she was ready, I breathed a sigh of relief. When we hung up the phone, I scheduled the appointment. I believed she was headed in the right direction. Unfortunately, Maria never returned after the first visit.

It can be challenging to watch someone you care for live a life of dissatisfaction, discontent, and unhappiness. While you try to do your best to support them, there are times you are just not sure you are making a difference. You feel a sense of helplessness. What do you do?

How do you support a friend or family member who you know is in a situation that is not in their best interest? You know they deserve better. You seem to want more for them than they want for themselves. While it may be difficult to listen to the same stories over and over, do lend an ear for support. Ask how you can support them specifically. Let them know that you are there for them. Be supportive of them and don't forget to take care of yourself in the process. Most importantly, keep in mind that they are responsible for their own change.

What is one thing you can do to support a friend or family member who is going through tough times?

who are you?

You can't be hesitant about who you are.

—VIOLA DAVIS

If someone were to ask, "Who are you?" what would your response be? Would you tell them who you are based on your roles, e.g., mother, father, grandmother, uncle, cousin, etc.?" Would your answer be reflective of what you do, e.g., lawyer, schoolteacher, physician, etc.?" Is your role or what you do the true essence of who you are? Finding the answer to this question is often one of mankind's lifelong pursuits.

At times, we can lose ourselves in our roles and responsibilities. The majority of our time is spent catering to the needs of others at the expense and neglect of ourselves. For example, while taking care of others is important and comes with being a parent, being mindful to carve out some alone time is just as important. For me, it's at night when everyone is in bed. I look forward to my time to reconnect with who I am.

What happens when you lose yourself in your relationship? Whether it's you focused too much on trying to please the other person or your desiring to belong and be validated was so great, you find yourself looking in the mirror and not recognizing the person looking back at you. You have lost a sense of who you are.

Rediscovering who you are can be enlightening and gratifying. Start by reflecting on those things that you may have enjoyed in the past that have now taken a back seat. Reintegrate them back into your life little by little. Part of rediscovering may involve trying new things, maybe something that you have always wanted to do but never got the chance. Spend time alone with yourself. Lastly, reconnect with who you are by identifying what you value and what matters the most to you. Remember, once you rediscover who you are, be true to yourself. Be true to yourself unashamedly.

Don't recognize who you are? Move toward rediscovery today.

chaos

*I'm thankful for my struggle because
without it I wouldn't have stumbled
across my strength.*

— ALEX ELLE

Many have described it as the calm before the storm. If you grew up in South Florida, hurricanes are all too familiar. Hurricane season begins in June and lasts through November. What's interesting about these natural disasters is that despite how devastating and destructive they can be, a day or two leading up to the storm making landfall, there is at times this calmness. The weather is beautiful. The sun is shining with not a cloud in the sky. If you were not aware a hurricane was on the horizon, you would never know based on the quietness and stillness in the atmosphere.

Hurricanes can be unpredictable. They may be forecasted to head in one direction and then shift and change course. Nonetheless, despite their unpredictable nature, you are provided time to make preparations. It's what you do with the time that matters.

Wouldn't it be nice to experience peace and tranquility no matter what is going on around you? To be able to go through life strong, tenacious, and resilient no matter the circumstance? I believe the answer is building strength in the quiet times in order to prepare for the difficult times. How does one do this?

One way to build resilience is to nurture your relationships on a continual basis. Maintain contact with your support when all is going well so that you have each other when faced with hardship. Build resilience by taking time to rest and restore, even when you are healthy and feel well. My suggestion would be to work hard for six days and to take one day of rest. Build resilience by minimizing your stress levels. Maintain a lifestyle that encompasses nurturing your physical, spiritual, and emotional health. Lastly, build resilience by getting back up again when you encounter obstacles. This builds confidence in your ability to overcome. The lesson, if you did it then, you can do it again.

What can you do today to build a more resilient you?

crossing bridges

Not everything that is faced can be changed,
but nothing can be changed until it is faced.

— JAMES BALDWIN

A bridge, a connecting, transitional, or intermediate route or phrase between two adjacent elements, activities, conditions, or the like. Many have become stressed out, fearful, anxious and overwhelmed when thinking about all of the "what ifs" in life. Why not try crossing each bridge as it comes? I know it is not always so easy, especially when you have a need to be in control or you're an overthinker, needing to cover all bases in an attempt to prevent problems and situations from arising.

What do we do if we are having difficulty crossing each bridge as it comes? When you find yourself anticipating problems, try bringing yourself back to the present and focus on the moment. There are effective ways to do this such as practicing meditation, breathing techniques, and relaxation. Take time to engage in these activities on a consistent basis; become familiar with them.

Be confident in knowing that as each bridge presents itself, you can make it to the other side. This may take a bit of reflection. That is, stay encouraged and focused by reflecting on the other bridges in your life that you have already crossed.

Access necessary resources and support and rely on them. Surround yourself with people who are positive, encouraging, and reassuring who can help to bolster your endurance and perseverance. Take them with you. You never know when you will need them to pick you up. You never know when they will need you to pick them up.

Remember that a bridge has a beginning and an end. It's transitional. Whatever problems or situations that lie ahead will not last forever. Stay focused on the present moment knowing with confidence that you will cross each bridge as it comes.

Remember bridges have a beginning and an end. Look ahead and stay focused.

alone time

Alone time is when I distance myself from the voices of the world so I can hear my own.

— OPRAH WINFREY

I did it on purpose. It was a selfless act. I'm guilty. I snuck away. I was alone but not lonely. While I enjoy spending time with my family and friends, I also enjoy spending time with myself. What about you? Do you set aside time to be alone? There are benefits.

Spending time alone allows us to restore and renew our physical, spiritual and mental well-being. It is in the solitude that we can assess where we are and where we want to go. Time alone helps us to pour into ourselves what we give to others. Show appreciation and gratitude towards self by spending time with yourself. Contentment will likely follow.

Solitude is necessary in order to appreciate the time we spend with others. We become better at appreciating others and enjoying our time together. Time spent alone helps us to refine ourselves to be the best version of ourselves. That's the gift that we not only want, but to present to the world as well.

This is a big one. Solitude guards against negative feelings of resentment and bitterness. We find ourselves giving to others and failing to give to ourselves. Resentment begins to creep in, especially when you see others taking their time. This often happens in relationships. One partner is good about taking time away to engage in what they enjoy. The other blames him or her for not getting their time. I challenge you to make yourself a priority and be intentional about scheduling your alone time and taking it.

Have you scheduled your alone time? If not, do it today?

wrapping it up

To my readers, it is my hope that *Moments of Mindfulness* has been thought-provoking, encouraging, and inspiring. My personal life experiences and professional work have enabled me to see a variety of different viewpoints and perspectives. From these encounters, I have gleaned practical tools that are effective and which transcend time, culture, and generations. Whether utilized as a 31-day reading, part of a book club, or a quick read at the beach or on a trip, I challenge you to delve in and allow *Moments of Mindfulness* to help you evolve into a better you. No matter where you are on your journey, I pray that *Moments of Mindfulness* will equip you to be intentional about your mental well-being, further enabling you to live a life of fervent purpose and abundant joy.

www.ingramcontent.com/pod-product-compliance
Lightning Source LLC
Chambersburg PA
CBHW051850040426
42447CB00006B/782